You Are a Smart Girl

by

Serah Chava

www.YouAreASmartGirl.com

Copyright © 2010, Serah Chava

All rights reserved

No part of this book may be reproduced or transmitted in any form or by any means, graphic, electronic, or mechanical, including photocopying, recording, taping, or by any information storage retrieval system, without the permission, in writing, from the publisher.

Fideli Publishing Inc.
119 W. Morgan St.
Martinsville, IN 46151
www.FideliPublishing.com

ISBN: 978-1-60414-282-2

Printed in the United States of America

Book Design: Bonita S. Watson

Dedication

    This book is dedicated to all the girls in the world who are smart, intelligent and responsible.

    To my wonderful students who made me realize that I can choose to walk away and yet return years later and say I wish I had stayed.

    You have given me purpose and will to keep on helping others.

    The commitment of the Tuck Foundation to remain with the girls until they succeed is extraordinary.

    Their work will continue to help and empower more girls.

Acknowledgments

Thanks so much to Jackie Schmall who was supportive of Smart Girls from the first moment she heard me speak about my work.In spite of her busy schedule as a writer,actor and producer she made herself available for valuable conversations,that helped focus the progress of the project.

Special thanks and acknowledgment to the Tuck foundation for their vision and works. Their purpose to keep on working harder,and smarter is admirable.

To all my friends and mentors thank you so much.In unique and wonderful ways,each one of you inspired me to continue the work.

Contents

Introduction ix
1　Media Influence............................... 1
2　Peer Pressure and Setting Goals 8
3　Sex.. 15
4　Weight Issues............................... 24
5　Self-Discipline and Self-Drive 29
6　Sexually Transmitted Diseases 43
7　Sexual Violence and Abuse.................... 49

Introduction

The purpose of this book is to teach and to guide both parents and girls on how to address and deal with issues that are being faced today; these are the challenges. As with any challenge, a solution has to be found. The solution is to build self-esteem and to create awareness.

Being in the classroom for the last ten months, I came to realize that it is very important that sex education be taught in schools. There is no specific curriculum. This book identifies the problems, teaches, and allows the learner room to grow. It also deals with current trends.

According to the National Campaign to Prevent Teen and Unwanted Pregnancy, statistics show that seventy-two percent of the girls between the ages of fifteen and nineteen will become pregnant and never finish school. Early learning is the best preparation (prevention is better than cure)

Let us look at the myths around sex and friends.

1. You cannot get pregnant the first time you have sex. MYTH. The answer is yes, you can, and it only takes seconds.
2. Having an older woman as a role model is a good idea. FACT. The answer is yes, and this is right. The wrong answer is no; she is too old for me.
3. Knowing why it is so important not to have sex before marriage will prevent early pregnancy, sexual transmitted diseases, HIV, and AIDS. FACT. For the parent, it gives a peace of mind.

When I started teaching these classes, one of the biggest objections came from the parents, who thought that the class was all about sex. With time, this is what l found out: Most parents were never taught about sex, and they are not teaching their children.

Your child being smart is one thing, but we all need to understand that we have so many smart, successful women who were victims of early pregnancy, incest, molestation, rape, drugs and sexual abuse. This book will prove you right that as a parent, you know how to raise your child

What this book does is to add onto this concern, to teach, and to direct. The need for this book has been more of the parents asking for it. My main goal is to reach more girls through teaching and writing. More parents have shown an interest in wanting to be part of it.

This book is built on the foundation and belief that every little girl has a heart: grow it, mend it, don't break it, and allow it to flourish. Inside every girl is an eagle; this eagle can learn how to fly if its wings are allowed to spread.

CHAPTER ONE

Media Influence

The media is the number one influence on girls today, followed by peer pressure. The media is a tool that is used to communicate and transmit information. It can be positive or negative.

Girls' Activities

- Draw a picture of yourself.
- Do not add anything that you do not have.
- Do not draw yourself as skinny you if you are not.
- List five things that you like about yourself.
- List five things that you do not like about yourself.
- What are some of the things that you feel you need to change to look better?

How do you feel about the following?

- Designer clothes
- Braces
- Long hair
- Making friends
- Weight issues

Parents, Guardians, Tutors

Discuss with your children about the answers and choices they have given. Show them that it is okay to feel insecure, but that it does not change how you feel about them. Love comes from within and you still love her regardless of how she looks or feels.

Many girls tend to feel down and isolated, especially if they are facing any of the above issues. Take the time to encourage her because otherwise she will keep on having these feelings.

It is okay to have extra weight; in some communities all over the world, beauty is embraced by women having additional weight. (We will tackle weight as a topic later in the book.)

BODY IMAGE AND THE WAY YOU SEE YOURSELF

Look at the person in the mirror and see if you like that person. You are all beautiful in many ways. It is not the outside that counts; it is the inside that matters. Beauty comes from within. How people view you on the outside is their own opinion. Carry yourself in a respectable manner all the time. Ignore bullies. When you respect others, you receive respect back. Ignore comments in the hallways; keep on walking.

Exercises

- List the type of shows that you watch and the reasons you watch them.

- List the types of magazines you read and the reasons you read them. How many times do you look at the cover of a magazine?
- Do you own an iPod or an MP3 player? Why is it so important to have one?
- What kind of clothes do you wear and why is it so important to you?
- Do you feel as if your friends have better things than you do? Would you like to have what they have?
- Who is your favorite role model and why? If you were to be given an opportunity to spend some time with one of your favorite celebrities, who would that be and why? Do you think this person is good enough or that her character is? Would you invite her to your school?

The media has a way of perfecting people's image by using makeup and altering photos. Trying to look like one of those girls in magazines or films is not something you should be doing. A smart girl builds her own image, self–esteem, and respect. Look at yourself and say, "I will make it and be better than everyone else is."

You can look up to very few young girls as role models in the media. If you can find one that is good, find out how she carries and conducts herself away from the cameras.

There are many older women in the media (with less publicity) that are good role models. Some of you have said that these women are too old for you. That could be, but the older generation can guide you and give you better advice. They have proved repeatedly that they have what it takes to make it in front of cameras. The question is can an older woman be a good role model?

SOCIAL WEB SITES

Social Web sites include Facebook, Twitter, and so many other sites that are not governed by parents. More and more girls are exchanging information with people they don't know. This is dangerous as it makes it easier for predators to prey on the children. The news media did a recent survey that shows that four out of five girls watched pornography while online doing homework. Online predators are a great threat; they know different tricks and acquire new trends.

What have you as a parent done to protect your children while they are online? How much freedom do you give your children? Remember these girls have a lot of knowledge, and they are proud to show it. As technology moves forward, more and more sites are being created, which makes it difficult to track them and your children.

Cell Phones and Text Messaging

Cell phone companies are now offering plans that offer unlimited text messaging, unlimited mobile-to-mobile calling, and a friends' list. This creates a big problem and should be a concern to everybody. Girls are text messaging all day. Information being passed on is deleted way before you get a hold of that cell phone. There are all kinds of social sites being texted to cell phones. Emails and text messages do not have a warning that says this is a minor.

So much text messaging takes place that people aren't paying attention to the roads. More and more young people are text messaging while walking; this can cause an accident.

Parents are buying these cell phones for the right reasons, but without proper monitoring, many companies are ready to get a hold of that phone for a financial gain, with ringtones, pictures, or games. They charge a separate fee, or include the additional fee in the plan. Some companies also send you texts without you communicating with them. Some of these messages contain obscene words and advertisements. Text messaging is now linked to health problems.

A lack of good-looking clothes or a cell phone should not be reasons you cannot respect peers or adults. A smart girl does not bring herself up while pulling others down. A new trend is that more and more people are talking on cell phones while carrying on additional conversations with those around them. What this means is lack of respect and a disregard for those around you. Respect orders and turn off the phone when asked to do so. Do not put others down because you have a cell phone or better things.

Exercise

Take the time to explain to your girls why you bought the computer and why they have those cell phones. Break everything down into features, advantages, and benefits.

It is easier to communicate and pass on information whenever needed with a cell phone. The benefit of this is that in case of an emergency, they can be reached, or they can reach you. Cell phones offer a sense of security where both of you can sit back and relax, knowing that everything is fine, and that should the need arise, you can all be reached instantly.

Cell phones are parents' eyes away from their children. Remind girls that they should not go beyond their minutes limit. Be sure to discuss who is allowed to call, whom they are allowed to call, and the times when the phone will be off. Set boundaries. Discuss whether or not it is okay for them to give out the phone number to friends and teachers.

Teenagers are been lured to sign up for certain services without parents' approval. What this means is that you end up getting a bill that you don't understand. Sometimes teens answer surveys online that request a phone number, and without understanding what it entails or by answering yes, these companies go ahead and charge a fee for something that no one understands or authorized.

To give you an insight into what some of these charges might be, let's look at what is being advertised and what is being left out. Most cell phones do advertise family-shared minutes and nothing else. With family plans, you can call five or ten friends without being charged. This is what they don't tell you: Those friends that you can call outside the network have to be in the system. You have to select those numbers when you sign up or go online and fill out the forms. Don't assume that this will automatically happen. If you call a number not in the system, you will be charged. As usual, get it in writing.

Text messaging is not free. You can buy a package depending on the company. It usually costs about ten cents per text message. Ring tones are not free; you have to purchase them as well. The music changes every month and so do the charges. All music is not billed the same; music that tops the charts is more expensive. Games are also billed separately. You can purchase a game to play for a certain amount of time. Charges differ. Surfing online incurs a charge. Receiving instant messages from favorites like E! News costs money. You will be billed to know where and what is happening with your favorite star.

Additionally, cell phones contain a lot of other charges that only those companies can explain. This increases the bill and you end up paying more. A bill that was initially set up for slightly less than one hundred dollars can go as high as double that if you agree to all of the above. It is one thing to purchase a cell phone for the purpose of using it for emergencies and being independent and end up not being in debt instead.

Alternatives to a fluctuating monthly bill that you can explore include prepaid cell phones, Virgin Mobile track phones, and Cricket, which offer free text messaging and unlimited minutes for as little as thirty dollars a month. These are just a few examples that can give you a piece of mind and freedom for your girls to text their friends as much as they want. There are no extra charges because you prepay everything. You can also get free phones. There probably many other companies that are cell-phone friendly and deliver the service as presented or requested.

Many see the family plans from T-Mobile as efficient and providing what is needed. AT&T is another company with family-friendly plans that allows communication between family and friends. They have excellent service and will forgive you in case you are late with your payment. Verizon wireless has promised delivery and keeps on getting better. They also have family and friends plans. As much as these companies advertise, you are the judge. You need to choose what is best for your family. Be wary of any other items that need to be purchased, as they might not come with the plan.

CHAPTER TWO

PEER PRESSURE AND SETTING GOALS

Peer pressure is the second highest influence in girls' lives. It is the reason more and more teenagers are falling victim to early pregnancy, sexual abuse, violence in dating, selecting the wrong friends, and wanting to dress a certain way.

Using friends to lie for you and with you to parents is wrong. A smart girl loves herself and only does what is right. Make friends with people to whom you can relate and who encourage you to be at your best all the time. Do not choose friends based on popularity, designer clothes, or lunch money. Do not strive to be a popular girl in school, but rather a smart girl. Tell your parents who your friends are. Those friends about whom you cannot tell your parents need to be out of your mind.

Peers are the reason most girls fall victims to alcohol and drugs, smoking, and abusing prescription medications. A drug like ecstasy is popular in teens' parties, dancing clubs, and nightclubs. Most of these drugs are colorless, odorless, and are added to beverages. This leads to rape, unwanted pregnancy, violence, and the spread of HIV and AIDS, and other sexually transmitted diseases.

Peers are now diagnosing other peers with symptoms and recommending medications. This has led to the use of medications for the wrong reasons.

Poor performance in school is sometimes caused by associating with peers who don't want to study or who are unruly and disrespectful

Most teenagers take the first cigarette because of peer influence. They are told how good and high it will feel, but they are not told about the consequences. Alcohol tastes terrible for someone who has not had a taste before, but around peers, there is so much encouragement that resisting temptation is not easy. Peers become advisers and will do what they know to cover up drug or alcohol use, or to help a friend with a hangover.

Many teens' accidents are associated with driving under the influence or being in a car driven by a friend who is drunk. Many will not say no, but will jump into the car without thinking about safety.

Every aspect of teenage girls is influenced by peers, from the clothes they wear, to shows they watch, to places they surf online, to the games in which they participate, from the type of cell phones they use, to the types of food they eat, and the restaurants they choose. There is so much pressure on girls today to be like their fellow girls at school. Some of these girls have learned from watching others, watching television, and reading magazines, and they decide what is appropriate and spread the word.

With new technology, communication is now fast and easy. Teenagers in today's world know much more compared to five years ago. Information travels fast.

We have two types of peers: Leaders and Followers

Leaders

These types of girls are the know–it-alls. They have ideas that might be good ideas, but they want it their way, and they want it now. They are leaders, and they expect every girl to follow them regardless of age. They are inventors and well versed with current trends.

Followers

Without question, followers are easily influenced by leaders. Peers have an upper hand in decision-making; even when these decisions don't favor them, they still follow. Followers tend to listen to peers much more than to teachers or to parents. To them, peers are always right no matter what. How much of an influence these peers are is not a concern of theirs.

Peers have become a source of information, decision-making, and solutions. Teenagers are spending a lot more time with peers than with adults and parents. They tend to seek, ask, listen, and trust their friends.

Activity

- Write down five names of your best friends.
- Write down five names of friends who are just friends.

Parent/Teacher Participation

- Discuss with your girls why they have two different sets of friends.
- Why some are just friends and not real friends?
- What don't they like about the second set of friends?

- If they could keep one list, are there some names that they feel they can do without?
- Explain the importance of eliminating certain names.
- Tell them to invite friends over so that you can get to know them.

Girls who are members of http://www.smartgirlclub8.com decided to drop certain friends who are not in the program because they realized they had nothing in common. Being a smart girl is about personal decisions and choices.

Striving to be Like or to Look Like Your Friends

You probably have friends who have designer clothes. What are you feelings towards not having designer clothes yourself? Do you feel it is very important to have designer clothes? What can go wrong if you do not have designer clothes? What would be better: a choice of designer clothes or saving for a college education?

In a survey, most of you said you probably won't wear clothes from certain stores. Asked what you would do if your parents bought you clothes that are not picture perfect, you answered that you would throw them in trash. Clothes with certain labels have a more appealing look and are more acceptable at school and with peers. Girls who don't wear designer clothes are looked at as cheap, and their families are labeled as financially grief stricken. Some girls pick on girls who don't wear designer clothes and make them feel down and beaten.

I want you to understand what designer clothes are all about and why you should not spent a minute worrying about not having them. Let's all go on a shopping spree together. We're going to the dollar discount store and we have a list of things to buy. Don't call this cheap because we are going to spend our money wisely. Here's what we're buying: a pair of jeans and t-shirt, bathing soap, shampoo and conditioner, washing detergent, facial cleansing products, towels, toothbrushes, deodorant, cologne, sandals, clothes, a prepaid cell phone, a handbag, CDs, books, candles, and a gift for your favorite teacher. The dollar store has both designer products and non-designer products. Shopping at a discount store gives you both more time and selection. It will give you all the products that you need without having to break the bank.

Even though these products don't have certain labels, we accomplished three things. First, we bought all the products we needed. Second, we saved money, which means we had money left over to establish a college fund. Third, we made smart choices. Originally, this was a class trip taken by a group of thirty girls. At first, they were little hesitant, but as the shopping progressed, they started participating more and were so excited to see that we buying good products and saving money.

There are many designers in the market, some that are known and some that are not known as well. You will be surprised that you may purchase quality products in some stores with a name that you have never heard before. Any time you see a name on television or in magazines, know that it is being advertised to increase sales. To find out how good a brand is, go online to consumers' reports. Some of these clothes have designers that go over and beyond to add glitter or anything to make them look fancy and cost more.

You can add accessories or glitter to clothes to make them look even better. Later in the book is a whole topic about recycling that should help you understand how to make and create things yourself. Learning how to make your own clothes it is an art and a good skill to posses.

Designer clothes or shoes do not change the person you are. They might be popular, but as mentioned previously, beauty comes from within a person. Ignore rude comments that people make to the contrary. You are also still too young to worry about looks. Let your parents help you decide what kind of clothes to wear.

SETTING GOALS

A goal is an objective or end that one strives to attain. Why is it so important to set goals? Do you have any goals?

Exercise

- Write down five goals.
- List these goals from most favorable to least favorable.
- Do you think you will accomplish these goals?
- What could hinder you from succeeding?
- If you were given an opportunity to go for these goals now, would you, or you would rather wait?

Every girl has goals in life. No matter their age, they all want to succeed. No child out there wants to fail. Failure comes because they did not do things the right way.

Yelling, and screaming are not the most effective ways to teach. Teaching creates success. Every girl has room to learn and to be the best. She also has a heart, so grow it and mentor it, but do not break it.

It is also very important to know that certain situations might hinder girls achieving their goals. One situation is pregnancy. Getting pregnant before completing school means dropping out to take care of the baby. Another situation is losing focus. A third situation that can hinder girls achieving their goals is hanging out with the wrong friends. A fourth situation is drinking alcohol and using drugs.

Let us look at different scenarios from the above examples. Scenarios two, three, and four are connected. Hanging around with friends who are involved in alcohol and drugs leads to experimentation, and as a result, a loss of focus (birds of a feather flock together).

On the positive side, hanging around the right company with good habits influences good behavior, and will lead to focusing on goals and studies.

Exercises

1. If you could change something about yourself today that might affect your goals, what would that be?

How strongly do you feel about the following activities?

2. Alcohol and drugs
   A. Shouldn't be involved
   B. Unsure
   C. Try alcohol and drugs
   D. No answer

3. Right choice of friends
   A. Parents should be involved in selecting them
   B. Parents should not be involved in selecting them
   C. Anyone can be a friend (no criteria)
   D. Unsure

4. Pregnancy
   A. Do not plan to get pregnant until married
   B. Not sure
   C. Not worried about it

5. Setting goals
   A. Not a concern
   B. I will set goals
   C. Unsure
   D. Not old enough

Have an adult look at the answers you have given and discuss them with you.

CHAPTER THREE

Sex

Of all the classes, this is a very important topic. This topic comes with a lot of questions and curiosity. While teaching it, you have to be very careful, precise, and straightforward on how you present every word and answer every question.

Introduction

Intercourse is when the head of the penis gets in contact with the vagina. The act is called sex.

When is it time to have sex? The appropriate time is in a marriage relationship when you are old enough and responsible.

What happens if teenagers have sex? A lot can go wrong from unwanted pregnancy and dropping out of school to care for the baby, to sexually transmitted diseases, HIV and AIDS. The problem is a world full of regrets.

Activity

- Have the girls write down what they think will happen if they became pregnant. (Most of the girls are in a position to answer and even mention peers who are having sex or who have had sex before.)
- List three names of teenagers you know who have become pregnant.
- What do you think will happen or what did happen to them?

Parent/Guardian/Teacher Participation

The answers provided above should not come as a surprise to you. Most of the girls listen to conversations or watch television and know what is going on. The best thing to do is to encourage them and to create awareness that they should not have sex before marriage.

Sex is not a very easy topic to teach, but it is very important to answer every question just as intended. Avoiding questions girls have is not helpful in the long run. There is need to revisit the subject periodically.

Abstinence is the key. Teach girls that they are beautiful from the inside. So many girls today have vowed to abstain from sex until marriage. Encourage your girls that they, too, can join these other girls. There is nothing wrong with them; they have selected a path that allows them to concentrate on set goals with no other distractions.

SEPARATING TRUTHS FROM MYTHS

- Having sex helps keep your boyfriend interested in you. MYTH.
- You cannot get pregnant the first time you have sex. MYTH. It only takes a few seconds.

- There is a difference between sexual feelings and love. TRUTH.
- Sexual feelings are normal and can be controlled. TRUTH.
- Pregnancy can occur anytime you have sexual intercourse. TRUTH.
- Only gay people get AIDS. MYTH. Anyone can get the virus if she has sex with an infected person.
- You will feel good about yourself if you do not have early sexual experiences in order to prove that you are a grown up. TRUTH. A smart girl takes a stand for what is right and builds character and self-esteem.

Discuss these myths with your girls. Separate the truths and help them to be understood. It might come as a surprise that even in these times these myths do exist. To get more help or to have trained teachers teach your girls, visit us at http://www.smartgirlclub8.com.

HOT BUTTONS

Smart girls build their own image, self-esteem and respect. Parents are part of the process, which enables growth. *You Are a Smart Girl* allows parents to be part of the learners' journey. We know how much you love your children and want the best for them. We do not challenge your authority, but we teach the entire positive aspects of life. We will prove you right.

PORNOGRAPHY

According to the news media, four out of five girls have visited pornography sites or looked at pornography while they were supposed to be doing homework. We will not be addressing pornography in this book, even though it might come up during a discussion. There is nothing to learn from it, and since it has a negative impact on society and morality, I only mention that girls are looking at these sites. Some questions might come up and the best thing to do is to let the girls know that you are here to learn positive things. Parental controls need to be on every computer that teenagers are using. Monitor what sites they visit.

DATING

Dating is the activity of going out regularly with somebody of the opposite sex as a social or romantic partner. What are the benefits of dating? Why do you think you need to date someone? When is the right time to start dating? What is the difference between going out with a friend and going out on a date? What is the right age to start dating.

Dating comes with a lot of responsibility. It is a choice and decision that you make. At fourteen years old some of you might be in a dating relationship already. You are still young. At fourteen years old, what do get by dating? This question was asked to a group of twenty girls, and the answer came back as nothing. The best thing is to wait until you are older.

A lot of things can go wrong with dating. Being away from adult supervision with a date can lead to the following problems: pregnancy, rape, transmission of diseases, violence, and the use of alcohol and drugs. So many cases that have turned tragic. A very common scenario is when things don't turn out to be as been expected and a girl is left without a ride. Getting into a car with a total stranger with the promise of a ride back home is jumping from the frying pan into the fire; it is very dangerous and just asking for trouble. The best thing to do is to call home. Calling people that you *think* you can trust with your safety might not be the best idea. Call a family member instead. You might not realize how vulnerable your life is. You need to be safe and there is nowhere safer than your own home.

Dating and Violence

Dating someone of whom your parents do not approve is a big mistake. Dating someone that your parents don't know is not the best decision, either. Give your parents a chance to meet this boy. Parents have a way of seeing things differently.

Recognize signs of violence. It starts off with demands, turns into verbal abuse, and then becomes physical. Many girls are in abusive relationships, and they choose to stay. Abuse never stops. The best thing is to discontinue that relationship. Perhaps the abuser needs more help. Someone who loves you cares about you; love is unconditional.

One specific case that has been in the media lately has left many girls wondering why this particular individual is still in the relationship. The media does not portray good role models. A smart girl respects herself and makes right decisions. Stay away from an abuser.

It is better for you not to be in a dating relationship at this stage, but if you choose to be in one, then the following will be of great help. Never be in a place alone with someone of the opposite sex. If you have to go somewhere, take a friend with you. Don't lie to your parents about where you are going and with whom you are going. Don't use friends to lie for you.

Be careful of a change of plans and tactics with which you don't agree. Everything needs to go as planned. And, remember that you have a curfew that you need to meet.

Have phone numbers of people that you can call if you need to call for help or for a ride. As with any unsupervised activity, common sense needs to be exercised all the time. Recognize controlling, abusive behavior. Abuse is abuse, whether it is physical, emotional, or verbal. The best thing to do is to get out of that relationship.

Don't listen to empty promises like, "I will change," or "I'll never do it again." People don't change that easily unless they take the steps to do it. Most of it is empty promises. Let them change for themselves and on their own clock, not on yours.

Abuse can occur over and over again and even turn tragic sooner or later. These are not stories, but real incidents that have taken place. Two mothers appeared on the TV show *Great Day Houston* to talk about their daughters being killed by boys whom they were dating.

Accept help from friends, parents, the community, church, or counselors who are able to guide and lead you in making good decisions.

STRESS

What causes stress?

Many factors can cause stress including family issues or problems at home with parents. School-related problems that might be due to low performance, getting in trouble, and fear of school can cause stress. Other sources of stress include feeling depressed, problems with peers, being bullied, breaking up with a boyfriend, moving to a new community, changing schools, chronic illnesses, unsafe living environments, and the family's financial problems.

What can you do to help your teenager daughter?

You can offer encouragement; there is no problem so big that one cannot overcome it. Give advice, but don't jump to conclusions. You can provide reassurance, support, and patience. Continue to provide structure and stability. Rules and goals must be followed; this is not time to lose focus.

Participation in sports and different kind of activities should be encouraged. Check your local listings to see what events are taking place in the community in which you can enroll your children. Discourage idle time. Visit friends; go to the movies and birthday parties. Build a good relationship with your teenager daughter so that she is comfortable coming to you with problems.

DATING ONLINE

These sites are off limits, as they have no parental supervision. They attract predators, child molesters, and so are dangerous. Communicating with someone you don't know puts you in harm's way. Girls are falling victim to many of these social networks even though there are warnings.

Developing a relationship with someone you don't know or haven't seen is more complicated. You cannot judge character over the Internet. There's no responsibility, but there are a lot of promises. Everything is bound to go wrong. Using webcams to communicate and posting pictures online exposes you to the wrong people. Pictures tell more than words; you will be surprised by how many people are watching you online.

The best way to determine character is to meet someone in person, and over a period of time, make a decision whether this is the right person by judging his character. You judge character through observation. Advertisements on television and online promise to match-make two people with two different backgrounds as being compatible. This is figured out is by comparing the dos and don'ts, the likes and the dislikes. As much as they say this works, we have the media reporting on how this kind of dating has turned out the wrong way.

Don't forget that you are online, and everything on the Internet is made to look glamorous. At no point do they tell you what kind of negative experiences they have had in the past. No two people are the same, and finding someone online cannot be easy, quick, and fun. You can do research online, but you cannot research character or ethics online. Anyone can post a picture-perfect profile of which none is true. I would encourage you to stop going to these sites; they are dangerous.

Exercise

- List four social sites that you have visited.
- Define chatting.
- What would attract you to go to these sites?
- Define the purpose of Twitter and Facebook.
- Have you thought about putting your picture online?
- What do you think about girls who post their pictures online?

Menstrual Cycle

Once a month, the uterus grows a new lining (endometrial) to get ready for a fertilized egg. If there is no egg, the uterus sheds its lining. This leads to bleeding, which is called a menstrual period. Girls usually start their menstrual periods between the ages of eleven and fourteen years old or as early as nine years old. This process only happens once a month. See a doctor if you notice any changes.

What Controls the Menstrual Cycle?

Hormones control your menstrual cycle. During each cycle, your brain, hypothalamus, and pituitary gland send hormone signals back and forth with your ovaries. The hormones estrogen and progesterone play the biggest role on how the uterus changes during each cycle.

Premenstrual Symptoms

For some, there is pain while others have no pain. Other symptoms may include feeling tense and angry, acne, gaining water weight, tender breasts, feeling bloated, having less energy, and cramps in your belly, back or legs. These symptoms usually go away in a day or two.

To help improve symptoms, exercise and eat a healthy diet. To relieve cramps, use a heating pad, hot water bottle, or take a warm bath. Use caution when taking over-the-counter medications, and make sure to discuss using such medications with a parent. Take a bath often and change your clothes. Be sure to use deodorants as well. To find out how to use feminine products, ask an adult to demonstrate. Most of the products do come with instructions that you can easily read, or you can ask a friend. Pads and tampons come in smaller sizes to keep in your pulse or bag to be used when the need arises or to help another girl.

Hygiene

Use pads or tampons that are available at the grocery store. Pads have adhesive strips and stick to your underwear. Tampons fit inside your vagina. These are perfect for swimming and other physical activities. They should be changed regularly.

Exercise

It is not necessary to see a doctor unless there is something unusual about your cycle. You should have a little calendar to write down the date that you have your periods. Take inventory of how many supplies you have or need. These include things like pads, tampons, deodorant, and cologne. Most of the hygiene products have coupons or sales that you can find at the stores, online, or in newspapers. This is where responsibility comes in. A smart girl is responsible and mature. Other changes that the body will experience include the growth of pubic hair and breast development.

Chapter Four

Weight Issues

Define the following words and answer the questions:

- Overweight
- Dieting
- Anorexia
- Bulimia
- Starvation
- What causes a person to be overweight?
- What is the media perception of people who are overweight?
- How does the public treat or perceive people who are overweight?

Media

Most magazines show pictures of skinny girls with perfect bodies. What they don't tell you is that these girls have been smeared with makeup to hide imperfections. What this does is to make many girls suffer from low self-esteem. Some have resorted to dieting, anorexia, bulimia, and starvation.

We have cases where some girls have starved to death. Food is needed by the body for various purposes. The body needs energy to function. Energy comes from eating healthy foods. Trying to look like the girls on television and in magazine creates a lot of health problems.

Look at yourself and see beauty from the inside. Just because you have extra weight should not make you feel less beautiful. Ignore negative comments and bullies. Be healthy by eating right and exercising.

Dieting

In a class of twenty girls, they revealed that they had tried the following diets or had family members on one of them: Slim-Fast, Weight Watchers, Jenny Craig, juice diets and skipping meals. Parents had also encouraged them to go on diets. Weight Watchers seemed to be the most popular. The girls in this class where ages eight to fourteen years old. Only three of the girls had real weight issues.

The best way to lose weight is to eat healthfully and to exercise regularly. Dieting at a younger age puts a lot of stress on the body. Skipping meals makes you lose concentration because you are hungry most of the time. You need to be more focused on studies and not on what people say about how much you weigh.

No girl should have a low self-esteem because of the way she looks. Carry on with your daily activities by ignoring people's comments. A smart girl makes good choices and decisions by not letting any outside influence affect her. She also takes a stand on what is right; this builds character and self-esteem.

Exercise

- List the types of food you like eating.
- List how many times you eat in a day and why you eat.
- What would happen if you did not eat?
- What would happen if you ate more food?

EATING DISORDERS

Anorexia Nervosa

Anorexia is a plan to follow a strict weight-loss diet. Limiting food leads to malnutrition and a general state of not being healthy. It also causes brain metabolism to change, a lack of appetite, and an inability to think clearly and make good decisions. Once anorexia starts, it poses a problem in returning to normal eating. It can continue for a long time if it is not treated. Death can occur due to starvation. People who are anorexic deny that they have a problem. They become socially withdrawn.

Some changes in behavior include eliminating certain foods that are perceived as high calorie such as meats and dairy foods. Exercising too much and making rules and rituals about food such as chewing it for a certain number of times are other behaviors that develop. Some anorexics develop a fear towards food and/or ignore their feelings of hunger.

Some complications that can occur include irregular heartbeat, depression, fatigue, lack of energy, absence of menstrual periods, constipation, abdominal pains, joint pain, and osteoporosis.

Bulimia

Bulimia is an eating disorder that involves bingeing on food followed by purging. It affects mostly women and teens. The symptoms include eating much more food than usual in a short amount of time (snacks, etc). This is called the binge cycle, and while it lasts, you feel that your eating is out of control. After bingeing, you try to control weight gain by vomiting, use of laxatives, diuretics, enemas or other medications, fasting, and excessive exercising. Body image and weight dominate your thoughts. People with bulimia have recurrent episodes of binge eating and purging. The weight fluctuation might be normal.

Some complications that can occur with bulimia include depression, tooth enamel erosion, gum infection, tooth discoloration caused by stomach acids from frequent vomiting, food cravings, and overuse of laxatives.

Emotional Eating

Sometimes, eating too much food brings comfort. In some cultures, food is a celebration. Some turn to food for emotional healing. What causes emotional eating? Emotional eating is caused by low self-esteem, stress, anxiety, frustration, depression, boredom, loneliness, and chronic anger. Social parties can lead to excessive eating due to encouragement by friends. Being at the wrong place at the wrong time, for example passing by a restaurant and smelling the food can cause emotional eating. Seeing food ads on television, combined with a lack of will power, and excuses leads to overeating as well.

Body image has become such a big fascination Hollywood and has been blamed by many as being the cause of some of these eating disorders. Some actors and actress have come out in the open to talk about their eating problems. More and more magazines show pictures of skinny girls who are depicted as beautiful. How beautiful can one be if she doesn't love herself from the inside? Not eating or binge eating is not beauty. This goes along with prescription medication, alcohol, and drugs.

Some television shows today are strongly against any kind of eating disorder. *America's Next Top Model* is one show that is very positive. At the same time, it showcases girls of all sizes. There is need for more of these types of shows to be aired. Girls need positive images and to see more girls who are not skinny. Extra weight in some communities is seen as a symbol of success.

If you think you are suffering from one of these eating disorders, seek medical attention immediately. Keep a journal of the foods you eat; this will help you to know how much you eat or need to eat on daily basis. Eating healthy and exercising regularly is the only way to lose and maintain weight.

Self-Esteem

Many girls experience low self-esteem. A number of factors can cause low self-esteem including peers, lack of friends, a sense of not belonging, competition, media influence, lack of role model, designer clothes, negative comments, and lack of moral support from family members and friends.

Ignoring what people say and taking a stand on what is right builds self-esteem. Selecting friends based on values will eliminate competition and encourage positive character. One of the ways in which competition creates low self-esteem is that there are some girls who are good at pulling others down while building themselves up. A good example is a girl who wants to be popular in school or to be the star. Being popular with no character does not create a good role model.

Negative comments being made by other girls should not bother you. Someone commenting about you weight or what type of clothes you wear should not lead into conflict. You are a smart girl who knows how to resolve conflict without violence. You have set goals in life to get good grades in school, not to make bad decisions, not to argue, to be a good role model, and to show respect to others. Taking a stand for what is right builds character and self-esteem.

CHAPTER FIVE

SELF-DISCIPLINE AND SELF-DRIVE

In this chapter, we will deal with the following topics: the generation gap and self-destructive habits.

GENERATION GAP

The gap between the young generation and the old keeps on increasing. Communication has somehow failed. The young are being viewed as disrespectful, as lacking in character, and difficult to learn. The young view the old as not listening or paying attention to them. This has resulted into both parties not understanding each other.

What is causing this gap? The generation gap is caused by a change of trends within the society, cultural and environmental barriers, lack of communication, and modern technology that is now easily available. The Internet has all answers that teens need.

Exercise

- List how many times you sit down and have a conversation with your child.
- List five things that you enjoy doing with your daughter.
- How often do you teach, correct, and direct? How is you tone?
- Do you do the following together: shopping, preparing meals, gardening, or visiting the school?

These exercises are very important because they will allow you to find out how much time you spend with your children. It will make you see in which areas you need to work and improve. It opens up a dialogue, which starts up a way of communicating. You cannot correct someone to whom you have no way of talking.

Every little girl has a heart; grow it and mend it. Communication is the key to close this generational gap. Girls at this age are knowledgeable and would like to share their knowledge. They are proud of who they are and have lots of energy. Develop a good relationship with your girl so that she is comfortable coming and talking to you.

Classroom Exercise

- List five things that would help you improve communication between you and adults, teachers, and parents.
- Do you think the adults around you listen when you talk?
- Do adults or anyone in authority have to listen to you or do you listen to them?
- If selected to participate in a forum on how to bridge this gap, what would you say?
- Do you speak while adults are talking?

Things that you can do to help bridge this generation gap: communicate, utilize good listening skills, show respect, avoid being in an argument, especially with an adult, make good decisions by deciding what is right and ask yourself if this is best for you.

Things that make the generation gap wider: feeling hurt and pain because you have been corrected or violated, taking a dangerous path to resolve issues, running away from home.

Running Away From Home

Why are more girls running away from home? Some reasons include lack of proper communication, being lured by friends through the Internet, school, or neighborhood, making a wrong decision, fun, abuse, molestation, rape, fear, low self-esteem, pain, hate for parents, not wanting to be told what to do, a promise of a better life, or searching for a better life.

Running away from home means a lot of things. This is a situation creates more problems than it solves and no one needs to be in it. You might end up at the wrong place with the wrong company.

What this company means is alcohol and drugs, pimping, child prostitution, rape, unwanted pregnancy, sexual abuse, physical assault, depression, and stress. It means being homeless because you have no job, money, or food. This has happened to a number of girls. Some have not been found because they ran away.

By setting goals in life, you can explore every positive means to make it. Running away is not a way to make it in life. Anytime you feel pain or hurt and you want to run away, contact someone who is in a position to help you. It should be an adult whom you can trust. The school has counselors to whom you can talk, and you can even talk to your teachers.

Hazing

What is hazing? Hazing is a ritualistic test and task that involves abuse, harassment, and humiliation. It is used as a way of initiating a person into a club, athletics, cheerleading, another group, or organization. There have been numerous reports on how humiliating and barbaric these acts have been. More and more girls are participating in hazing or have been victims of it.

Hazing usually involves acts like sleep deprivation, alcohol consumption, or sex acts, which are a common practice. Question: will you participate in hazing?

Why does hazing go unreported? People don't report hazing incidents because of a commitment to pledges, beliefs, loyalty to the group, and feelings of being embarrassed. Only you can end hazing by speaking up and reporting the incidents.

PREVENTING PREGNANCY

Pregnancy has its own responsibilities. The best thing is to wait until you are married to become pregnant. Being pregnant as a teenager should not even been in your mind. Abstain from sex.

I will not be addressing how not to get pregnant because you are a smart girl who feels good about yourself. You know not to have early sexual experiences to prove that you are a grown up.

Lately, there has been a debate on the media about the morning after pill. This is not for you. Why not? You are a still young; you have set goals in life to achieve good grades in school and go to college. Early pregnancy leads to dropping out of school. This pill does not in any way protect you against sexually transmitted diseases, HIV, or AIDS. It is a drug that has side effects. It is a door that if left open, leads down a wrong path.

DRIVING AND DRINKING

Do girls who drink alcohol have more friends? According to the Highway and Traffic Safety Administration and http://www.duihelpers.com, a drunk driver kills someone every thirty-nine minutes in the United States. Eight teenagers die daily in alcohol-related car accidents. Let us look at two types of scenarios and make a decision

Select the best answer possible to the following question: Which of the following is not a concern to you?

A. Thinking that you are not drunk and getting behind the wheel
B. Being in a car driven by someone under the influence
C. Both
D. Not sure/don't know/none

Driving while drunk is dangerous because alcohol causes impairment and you cannot make decisions when you are drunk. It also slows judgment and reaction time. It is irresponsible and has severe consequences. Don't drink and drive. Seek help or call someone to come take you home. This call has to be made to people whom you trust or whom you know very well.

Getting into a car that is being driven by someone under the influence or whom you suspect is drunk is just as dangerous as driving under the influence yourself. You are both at risk. If you suspect that someone is under the influence and she wants to get behind the wheel, alert authorities immediately.

OTHER DISRUPTIONS WHILE DRIVING

These disruptions make for unsafe driving conditions: talking on the phone, text messaging, tuning the radio to different stations, speeding, and not obeying your parents' rules.

Pull over to the side of the road if you need to text message or make a phone call. If the phone call is not life threatening, it can always wait. Following rules set by parents when it comes to driving ensures safety. Take a driver's education class to promote safe driving. Respect the roads, and you will get home safely and not be in trouble with the law
SAFE DRIVING BEGINS WITH YOU.

TATTOOS

A tattoo is a form of body art. It can be permanent or temporary. Some tattoos are used for medical reasons and might not be decorative. Cultural tattoos are applied to members of certain ethnic groups for ritual purposes, cosmetic purposes, or for functional purposes.

What causes people to have tattoos? Some reasons include to look beautiful, to show a group symbol, to pass a message, to show toughness, to show love and loyalty (by getting a tattoo of a friend's name, for example).

Types of Tattoos

Amateur tattoos are usually done by individuals and friends with a pin and ink, although charcoal or ashes might be used. They are unprofessional and pose as a high risk for infection. Professional tattoos are usually done by someone who is registered and licensed and uses the right kind of sterilized equipment.

Risks

HIV and Hepatitis C can spread from use of unclean needles. Other risks include deep skin infections, allergic reactions, tissue injuries, and inflammatory infections. Even though tattoos can be removed, the skin might not return to its original color.

Socially, too many tattoos—especially in highly visible places—create attention. It might also pose as a problem to getting a job. Financially, it is expensive to remove tattoos.

SMOKING

Is it okay for girls your age to smoke cigarettes? Tobacco contains nicotine, which acts as a stimulant. When the body becomes accustomed to the presence of nicotine, it requires the use of chemicals to help it function normally. This level of dependence is referred to as addiction. Nicotine raises the levels of neurotransmitters called dopamine in parts of the brain to produce feelings of pleasure.

Cigarette smoking is dangerous to the body. It causes lung cancer. It acts as an appetite suppressant, and some people think that it relieves stress.

Situations that might increases chances of smoking include being around the wrong company (selection of friends is very important), unsupervised slumber parties, social gathering, and parties. Weekends full of idle time, advertisements, and commercials also contribute to people starting to smoke. Some people start smoking for fun as a recreational activity or to try to lose weight.

Question: which is more harmful, smoking less or smoking more?

There is no safe amount of smoking; smoke attacks living tissues, which leads to smokers having less ability to carry oxygen to the rest of the body.

What happens when one smokes cigarettes? Smoking changes skin elasticity, and fine lines appear around the eyes and mouth. Respiratory infections, coughs, colds, sinus infections, sore throats, and ear infections multiply when one starts smoking. These infections are as a result of damage to cilia in the lungs. Cilia are tiny parts of the lung that clear out bacteria, viruses, and dirt. When they stop functioning, germs and dirt accumulate, resulting in more frequent and longer lasting colds. Smokers have less endurance, which affects participation in sports.

How to Stop Smoking

The first thing about smoking is never to touch a cigarette. Never start smoking. To stop smoking, you have to motivate yourself. You need self-drive and inward motivation. Don't let repeated, failed attempts hold you back from trying to quit again.

A SMART GIRL TAKES RESPONSIBILITY FOR HER ACTIONS.

Drug Abuse

A drug is any substance other than food that changes the function or structure of the body or mind when ingested. How much one takes determines the effects of the drug. A small amount acts as a stimulant; a greater sedative can be a larger poison and can kill.

Addiction is physiological, emotional, and psychological dependence on a substance such as alcohol or drugs that has progressed beyond voluntary control. Drug abuse is the use of illegal drugs or inappropriate use of legal drugs. It is also the repeated use of drugs to produce pleasure, alleviate stress, alter or avoid reality.

The media is a big influence in promoting drug abuse, along with peers and medical professionals who don't abide by the law or value moral ethics. As much as we all love to go the doctor when we fall ill, we need to be cautious about what kind of doctor we visit. Your overall health is very important, and as mentioned previously, you have to be careful about what goes into your body. If you allow anything to go inside of your body, it will have its effects on you, not on the person who gave you the substance. The same thing goes for alcohol, smoking, sex, and the spread of HIV, AIDS, and other sexually transmitted diseases. Make sure that you are checked and treated by professionals in a licensed facility such as a hospital or well-known doctors' office.

Don't self-diagnose or take medications on your own, but only as instructed by the doctor. This is what happens a lot of times when medications leave the pharmacy or the doctor's office. In 2006, the United States Department of Health and Human Services carried out studies that showed that 2.1 million children ages 12 years and older have used prescription medication for non-medical purposes in the last 30 to 60 days.

There is also an increase in abuse of prescription medications in the United States. Some drugs are easily available on the streets and have various names like huffing and sniffing. How these medications are getting on the streets becomes a big hurdle to crank. If you come across someone trying to sell you any kind of drugs or prescription drugs, report it to the authorities. The hardest part is not to allowing them or the drugs to be on the streets where they're likely going to kill someone else. Any suspicious activity also needs to be reported.

Prescription Drugs

Prescription drugs have the potential to be just as harmful as street drugs are. What is the media's role when it comes to prescription drugs? Let's discuss various types of drugs, their effects, and how to stay drug free. Prescription medication is prescribed by a doctor. Over-the-counter medications are those that you can buy at the pharmacy store or drug store without a prescription.

The types of prescription medications that are being abused include Ritalin, oxytocin, Vicodin. A growing number of teenagers are taking these drugs for non-medical use.

Over the counter medications being abused include cough syrups such as Nyquil, Robitussin, and Vicks. Dextromethorphan is found inside the syrup.

Why are teenagers taking these drugs? They are taking them to get high for recreational purposes, to decrease appetite, and to compensate for a lack of sleep.

Some of the consequences of taking unneeded prescription drugs are addiction, irregular heartbeat, nervousness, and heart failure.

Prescription Stimulants

These are a major category of abused prescription drugs. These drugs are almost exclusively prescribed for Attention Deficit Disorder (ADD), Attention Deficit with Hyperactivity Disorder (ADHD), and narcolepsy. Teenagers take them to increase energy, for mental alertness, and awareness. Ritalin is nicknamed the smart drug. College students are known to take this drug to make them stay awake all night to study.

How do the media make it easy for people to get information or drugs? Numerous advertising campaigns on television say what a particular drug does and how to get it. Street smarts know where these drugs are easily available on the street and Internet links provide information and purchasing.

Drug Enablers

Enabler number one: fellow peers who play a doctor's role by diagnosing and prescribing certain medications.

Enabler number two: the Internet. All one needs is description of the symptoms (which might not exist) plus a credit card. Prepaid credit cards are easily available at the grocery store. With ten dollars, it is so easy to open an account and keep on adding money.

Now that you realize how easy it is to get drugs and how easy it is to get hooked on them, answer the following question. Do girls who take drugs and drink alcohol have more friends?

How to Stay Drug Free

Don't self medicate. Go to doctors because they have medical training and experience to determine which drugs are safe and healthy. More teens are now asking doctors to prescribe certain medications for them.

Someone who cares about your health will do what is right and will not become an enabler. Be careful of certain doctors. As we talked about with sexually transmitted diseases, going to the hospital for tests is better than going to someone down the street.

Just as with teaching, teachers follow a strict syllabus. What would happen if teachers taught only what you want to learn? Selecting the proper friends and making right decision need to be your primary goals. As time moves on, getting drugs is as easy as ABC. This problem keeps on getting bigger and closer to home.

There are a number of drugs being used in teen parties, nightclubs, and dance clubs. Ecstasy is one of them. These drugs are colorless and tasteless and can be added to beverages without one noticing. This creates a much higher risk of date rape, which can spread HIV, AIDS, and other sexually transmitted diseases.

Street drugs are found nearly in every corner of the street. These are inhalants that have street names like sniffing, and huffing. Some household items are being inhaled to produce a pleasurable feeling. This causes serious respiratory problems and permanent brain damage. Drugs are associated with increased risk of drug use later on in life. It leads to poor performance in school, poor judgment, and a risk of accidents. Other risks include violence, unplanned pregnancy, and unsafe sex, which spreads HIV, AIDS, and other sexually transmitted diseases.

When it comes to drugs, the best thing is not to even take the first step. There is nothing promising about drugs. Peers' promises of getting high or feeling good are not what you should believe. Now you have the necessary information about drugs. Other girls will tell you how good a drug is or what it can do for you, but they never will tell you what the consequences are. Before taking the first smoke, take a tour to the hospital and let the doctor show you and explain real life examples. Do the same thing with drugs: visit a street corner full of addicts and picture that lifestyle. No, that is not for you.

SAY NO ALCOHOL; SAY NO TO DRUGS; SAY NO TO SEX BEFORE MARRIAGE. Taking the first step leads to a dangerous path in life.

Damage to the Skin

Sun Exposure

Sun exposure causes most of the changes and discolorations to the skin. The sun ultraviolet (UV) light damages the fibers on the skin called elastic. When these fibers break down, the skin begins to sag, stretch, bruise, and tear more easily. This damage might not be visible at a younger age.

Ultraviolet radiation from the sun is the number one cause of skin cancer. UV light from tanning is also harmful. Exposure to sunlight in the summertime and in the wintertime puts you at the same risk.

To prevent the skin from damage, limit the amount of time you spent outside. Apply a sunscreen every time you go out. Wear protective sunglasses and hats. Visit a dermatologist at least once a year.

Acne

Acne occurs when there is a buildup of dead skin cells in the pores. Facial breakouts are more common in teenagers. Acne is usually related to increased sebum production. Sebum is an oily substance naturally produced by the skin. Excess sebum can mix with dead skin cells that build up in pores, resulting in a clogged pore. The sebum in clogged pores promotes the growth of bacteria. This leads to the inflammation that is associated with pimples.

Treatment

There are a number of dermatologist-developed products that both treat and prevent breakouts to give you clear, healthier skin. Develop a skin regiment to clean your face every night before going to bed. How to clean the face: use cold water, then warm water, and then finish with cold water.

Let's See How Well We Are Doing

At this point, if you are a parent, guardian, teacher, or volunteer working with a student or students, it is important to know if learning has taken place. The whole idea of this book is to allow the parent or any other person teaching to have close interaction with the learner(s). You can choose to proceed to the next chapter, but always come back. I hope you have all learned something. Let's take a look and review some of the things we have learned and what has happened.

First Lesson

The goal was to build self-esteem. Be more involved and try to understand the student from her own perspective. The first exercise was for the girls to draw a picture of themselves. In a class of twenty girls, only three drew a real picture of themselves. They altered or added something that they did not have. Why? Because that is the way they wanted to look.

What was added? Short hair was replaced with long hair, short nails with long nails, and accessories like hair clips were added. Ponytails were taken down. Clothes were altered to look picture perfect. Most girls drew a picture that made them look skinny. Weight was a concern, and they we not willing to accept that they had more weight than what the picture showed.

Only three girls were skinny. Two accepted that they had weight problems, and it caused low self-esteem. The same two girls also wanted help. Beauty comes from within. All the girls were beautiful, eager, and willing to learn.

Weight

In a class of twenty girls, the question was how does one lose weight? Answer: diet, eat less, Jenny Craig, Weight Watchers, and Nutrisystem. When asked how they know about the above diets, they said family members, television, friends, and magazines.

What about exercise and eating healthy? Some did these things, while others only exercised at school. A few girls had an exercise routine and were motivated to continue since their families were active in sports and regular exercise.

Media Influence and Role Models

This was the most fascinating topic. Big and small names came up as well as what they liked about their favorite stars. Certain names were adored even though none of them was a role model. They loved products that came with certain names like cologne and clothes.

Most girls wanted to look like the girls in magazines. Asked whether an older woman could be a good role model, the answer was unsure, no, or an older woman is too old to relate to. There is need for the media to portray good role models for the girls. Most of the girls on television or magazines are not good role models.

Goal Setting

Everybody had goals. Some of these goals were terrific. They all wanted to succeed. This shows you that every girl has room to succeed.

Online Chatting

Some viewed this as a good thing as they could keep in touch with friends. The only problem was lack of understanding about how dangerous online chatting can be. Girls didn't know how secure their home computer was. Four of the girls said their parents made it very clear how they needed to use the computer. The same girls had software installed on their computers to protect them. They were fine with it.

These are just a few of the classroom reviews. As you might have seen, no girl out there wants to fail. Society creates failure through statistics and ignorance, but it also takes the society to mend and grow.

CHAPTER SIX

SEXUALLY TRANSMITTED DISEASES

Different Types of Diseases

Sexually transmitted diseases are infections that are transferred from one person to another through sexual contact. More than twenty-five diseases are transmitted through sexual activity. Every year, nineteen million infections attack people between the ages of fifteen and twenty-four.

Let's look at the following infections and how they affect health: gonorrhea, syphilis, herpes, chlamydia, trichomoniasis, human papillomavirus, hepatitis B, HIV, and AIDS. They all have severe consequences. They can be fatal and can also cause pelvic inflammatory diseases, which can cause infertility.

Gonorrhea and Chlamydia

They all infect at the same time. Untreated gonorrhea spreads to the uterus and the fallopian tubes. Some symptoms of gonorrhea include abnormal bleeding, a burning sensation during urination, vaginal discharge, and general irritation of the outer area of the vagina. Some symptoms of chlamydia include vaginal discharge, pain while urinating, light vaginal bleeding, vaginal bleeding after intercourse, smelly, yellow vaginal discharge, and lower back and abdominal pain that is worse during the menstrual cycle.

Syphilis

Symptoms of syphilis include painless, open genital sores, vaginal ulcers, mouth ulcers, vaginal warts, flu-like symptoms, skin rash, mild fever, fatigue, headache, sore throat, muscle aches, and a loss of appetite.

It can easily be treated. Without treatment, symptoms can progress and affect the nervous system and the brain. It can also lead to dementia and death.

Herpes

Herpes has no cure. Some of the symptoms include blisters and sores that periodically break out in the genitals.

Trichomoniasis

It is a commonly curable sexually transmitted disease. Its symptoms include frothy, yellow-green discharge with a strong odor and lower abdominal pain that usually appears between five and twenty-eight days after exposure.

Human Papilloma Virus

This virus is thought to be one of the main causes of cervical cancer. It is also linked to some other cancers of the female reproductive system. Human Papilloma Virus can be treated to reduce its signs and symptoms. There is currently no cure. There is a vaccine developed to prevent the virus.

Hepatitis C

Both hepatitis A and C can be passed through sexual contact. Once infected, there is no cure. The symptoms of hepatitis C include flu-like symptoms, fever, fatigue, nausea, vomiting, loss of appetite, abdominal pain, diarrhea, jaundice, light-colored stools, and darker urine.

HIV and AIDS

Many people are worried about getting HIV. There a numerous advertisements and campaigns that educate people about the disease. This is one area where the media has come up in a more aggressive and positive way. We have billboards on display and radio stations always encouraging people to get tested. Countries like South Africa have literature and warning signs about the disease posted in every street corner. This creates awareness and reminds people of how life-threatening HIV is.

HIV, which stands for Human Immunodeficiency Virus, is a viral infection that affects present cells in the human blood system, semen, and other bodily fluids. It is passed primarily through vaginal and anal sex. The infection affects the body's immune system. This makes it difficult for the body to fight diseases and infections because the T-cell lymphocytes (infection fighting cells) have been destroyed. An infected person is highly susceptible to illnesses that her body would otherwise be able to fight off. It is also transmitted at birth if the mother is infected. Those who acquire HIV often develop AIDS (Acquired Immunodeficiency Syndrome).

Let's look at some of the symptoms of HIV. Between six weeks and three months after becoming infected with the HIV virus, the body develops flu-like symptoms, a fever, a rash, muscle aches, swollen lymph nodes and glands. Other symptoms include chronic yeast infections on the mouth, fever or night sweats, easy bruising, bouts of extreme exhaustion, unexplained rashes, appearance of purplish lesions on the skin or inside the mouth, sudden, unexplained weight loss, and chronic diarrhea lasting one month. People infected with HIV can expect to develop AIDS in about eight and ten years. At this point, symptoms become more severe.

Symptoms of AIDS include pulmonary tuberculosis, recurrent pneumonia, severe bacterial infections, invasive cervical cancer, lymphoma, Kaposi's sarcoma, candidacies of the esophagus, bronchi, or lungs, vision loss, nerve damage, brain impairment, trouble thinking, loss of co-ordination, lack of balance, and behavioral changes.

More that forty million people are infected by HIV and AIDS worldwide. Fifty percent of those infected are women. In United States, sixty-five percent of the new cases are teenagers. African Americans represent fifty percent of the population. Twenty percent of African American women are more likely to acquire the deadly virus than white women are. Hispanics have the second highest population with HIV and AIDS. This information is from http://www.avert.org.

Separating Truths from Myths about HIV and AIDS

There is no cure for AIDS. There are medications available which can slow done the infection and prolong lifespan. The HIV virus is transmitted through vaginal and anal sex. It can also be transmitted through blood by the sharing of needles. A person might look healthy but still have the virus. It is not true that only gay people are infected by AIDS. The only way to know if someone has AIDS is by being tested. Tests have to be done at the hospital or by licensed laboratories.

Answer the following questions:

1. Only gay people have AIDS.
   A. true
   B. false
   C. unsure

2. Sexual feelings are normal and can be controlled.
   A. true

B. false
   C. unsure

3. A person might look healthy but still have the virus
   A. true
   B. alse
   C. unsure

4. There is a difference between sexual feelings and love
   A. true
   B. false
   C. unsure

5. How do you know if you have AIDS?
   A. by asking friends
   B. finding answers online
   C. being tested

6. How long does HIV virus take before developing into AIDS?
   A. six weeks to three months
   B. immediately
   C. eight to ten years

7. Do you think you will be sexually active?

8. How many times have you had sexual intercourse in the past week?

9. Before dating someone, would you ask him to be tested?

10. If yes, what would be an ideal place for you?

11. Write down five symptoms of HIV.

12. Write down five symptoms of AIDS.

Conclusion

In this chapter, we covered prescription drugs and sexually transmitted diseases. Alcohol, drugs, and prescription medications are becoming more and more common. They are easily found in cabinets around the house or at the pharmacy store. Respecting prescriptions is the key even when the label says it can treat the symptoms that you have. If it was not prescribed for you, it is dangerous. Most doctors do a physical before treating a patient.

Sexually transmitted diseases are on the rise among teenagers. Many of these symptoms might come and disappear, but if not treated, they still pose a risk. Seek medical attention immediately. Don't try to self-medicate.

The most important thing is self-discipline. Having early sexual experiences is not the way to prove that you are a grownup.

CHAPTER SEVEN

SEXUAL VIOLENCE AND ABUSE

This chapter deals with sexual abuse, violence, sexual assault, rape, incest, and sexual molestation. What do you do if you are confronted with any of these problems?

RAPE

Rape is also referred to as sexual assault. It is the act of forcing someone to have sex without that person's consent. It is a crime punishable by law.

There are different types of rape. The attacker uses both force and violence or threats to take control over the victim. Use of drugs to take away the person's ability to fight back. Alcohol and drugs have been used on rape victims in what is called date rape by a boyfriend.

What can you do to protect yourself? Before an attack, rapists always try to find a comfort zone. They study and know the surroundings. They even map out areas to which they can take their victims. These are usually isolated areas, abandoned buildings, bridges, vacant lots, car garages, dark streets, etc. The first thing to do is to try to free yourself by kicking, biting, pulling, or hitting by using anything available. Do not allow the attacker to progress towards this comfort zone. This comfort zone gives him more advantage and control. Chances are that he will carry out his wishes. It is like falling from a frying pan into the fire. If he has a weapon, your best bet is to fall down and pretend to be dead.

The only person who can protect you is yourself. Maybe you have heard this many times, but more and more rape cases are being reported daily. Those who survive make it by fighting the attacker by all means possible.

You need to know your environment. If you are visiting a place for the first time, it is never a waste of time to study or ask questions about the area. Knowing the environment is a protection by itself. Never be alone in a place. If you have to, ask a friend to accompany you. If you are walking alone, never allow someone to walk behind you or pass someone too closely; give yourself a big distance while passing someone on the street, especially if you are the only two people walking. Walk on streets that have lights where someone can see you. It is good to change your daily routine so that someone watching does not know your moves or timing. Bear in mind that rapists can still attack at the doorstep especially if they know your daily routine and route. Be cautious while approaching a building or getting off the bus; if you see someone suspicious; don't head on home. Follow the other kids to their house. Call home from there for an adult to come and get you.

Rapists have different motives and a different ways of thinking. They could be they type of rapist to rape and leave, or the type to rape and stay. We have seen cases of many children being abducted and taken away. That is why you cannot trust what your attacker tells you in case you cannot free yourself. Fight the fight to freedom; without freedom, you are and always will be a victim.

What should you do if you are raped? Rape is not your fault. Medical attention needs to be attained right away without washing, taking a shower, or changing clothes. This will help ensure that you get proper care. Report it to the police. Don't seek to protect the perpetrator, especially if you know him. He might rape someone else. Let the law deal with it. This is also the beginning of the healing process. Seek help from counselors at school or call the national assault hotline at 1–800–656–HOPE.

How does rape affect the victim? Most rape victims become confused, angry, embarrassed, ashamed, depressed, anxious, nervous, frightened, and withdrawn from family members and friends. They also suffer from flashbacks and nightmares.

Incest

Incest is having sexual intercourse between close family members. Socially, it is a taboo; it is also illegal. Family members usually include father and daughter, brothers, cousins, etc. Incest takes place more than it is reported. It is something that victims keep between themselves and family members. It's usually a closely guided family secret. Most victims of incest suffer through the pain for years because of fear of the attacker, especially if they are young. The attacker threatens that if they talked about it they would be harmed or the whole family would. There is also fear that no one would believe them or it is their fault. Incest can go on for years. It usually starts at a young age, and the victim is made to believe that it is the right thing to do. Families would rather ignore the issue and not talk about it.

Healing has to start from within a person. Unlike rape, which might be one attack, incest victims might have endured years of abuse, even though this might not be the case with everyone. Sexual assault, abuse, and molestation leave painful scars if they are not treated both emotionally and physically

Going Green

Why do we have to go green? We all need to save and preserve our natural resources for future generations. We can achieve this by saving fuel sources, and keeping our soil and air clean.

The number one threat to the environment is man. By digging and cultivating, man has continued to rid the environment of its natural resources. Other acts include dumping trash in rivers and lakes, cutting trees without planting new ones, and pollution.

Things that we throw away can affect the environment. Batteries and other household items like electronics contain dangerous chemicals. If they are buried in the soil, they leak through the bottom barrier and pollute the ground water. This contaminates the water and the soil in which food grows.

How can you help? Recycle, for starters. Recycling helps to save energy, water, and natural resources. Recycling one glass bottle saves enough electricity to power a 100-watt bulb for four hours. Recycling one ton of paper saves over 7,000 gallons of water, 380 gallons of oil, and enough electricity to power an average house for 6 months. It also saves by not cutting down forests, and prevents soil erosion. Recycling one aluminum can helps to save enough power to run a television for six hours. Reduce your power consumption by turning off lights in areas not used and setting your thermostat a few degrees lower in the winter and a few degrees higher in the summer to save on heating and cooling costs. Unplug electrical appliances when not in use (hair dryers, etc.). Replace your old bulbs with compact fluorescent light bulbs. Wash clothes in cold water if possible since eighty-five percent of the energy is used is to heat water in the washing machine. Air clothes in the open or add a dryer ball in the dryer to cut down on drying time.

Practice responsible water usage. Never leave the tap running. Take responsibility and turn off running water in public places. This wastage costs everybody time and money and is harmful to the environment. Take shorter showers to reduce water consumption and heating costs. Purify water by using a water filter; this will save on buying bottled water and container use. Plant a garden to provide fruits and vegetables. If possible, select drought-tolerant, native plants that need less water. Don't flush sanitary pads in the commode. Save gas and improve your health at the same time: walk or bike; walking improves cardiovascular and reduces the risk of obesity.

Bulk buying from stores like Sam's Club and Costco leaves more money in your pocket and cuts down the costs of packaging. Utilize friends to find affordable quality products that will last longer. Find resale shops and garage sales. Sell products that you don't need to reduce clutter.

Borrowing items from neighbors or friends helps save money, especially if you only need them for a short amount of time. Remember to be good neighbors take back what you borrow.

Recycle electronics or keep them longer. With new technology, we have new products on the market every day. Many people are now keeping their cell phones for a short amount of time. Recycling is the best thing to do.

Some products can be made at home with basic ingredients like lemon, vinegar, and baking soda. You can easily make soap or candles without having to buy very expensive ingredients.

Enroll in a cooking and sewing class. Learn how to cook; it is a good skill. Feeding neighbors and friends or cooking for the family is a good way to show appreciation for those whom you love. Knowing how to sew cuts down on how many trips you make to the mall. All these are good skills to have.

Homework

Does your community or school have a recycling project? If not, would you be willing to ask those in authority to start one?

Knowing the benefits of recycling, would you participate in it more or teach others about its benefits?

It is very important to know that recycling starts with you; it is the little things that you do that matter the most. In essence, you carry the key to making this environment better. This environment needs you just as much as you need it.

Things around the house that you can recycle include old CDs; these can be recycled to decorate or used on the sidewalks as reflectors. They can act as centerpieces on table displays and festive designs for Christmas. You can create wallpaper designs, borders, and blinds. Tuna cans and cat food cans can be turned into holiday candy containers. Paint the cans in different colors and cover with ribbons, which you can easily find at resale stores, to make them more decorative. These can be nicely wrapped and given out during Christmas or for birthdays. Plastic cases that come with CDs can be recycled or reused. Paint your favorite glass designs inside or on top of the case. Attach a magnetic strip on the back of the case and use them as picture frames on the refrigerator.

Bend wire hangers into different shapes and designs to make candy wreaths for Christmas or any other holiday. Wrap pieces of candy and tie ribbons around them to attach them to the shapes. Wire hangers can be used for Halloween decorations in the yard. Hang them on the tree for Christmas decorations.

Layer old newspapers to use for insulation for heating and cooling. Stuff rolled up newspapers under the door cracks or in window cracks. This will act as insulation. Stuff them under coats or blankets to keep warm in case of an emergency. Old newspapers are great for working surfaces while painting, doing crafts, or decorating. They work well for polishing and shining glass after washing windows with regular cleaner. They can be an odor remover for shoes (stuff into shoes at night), plastic containers, and luggage. Old newspapers can be used as mulch in the garden. Spread them flat or shred them around the base of the plants or between rows of plants; this will discourage weeds from growing. Old newspapers are used for packaging and fire starters. They can keep the shape in boots, luggage, and purses. You can use them to make dress patterns while making your own clothes. They can act as a sponge to clean grease from stove and other places.

Surfing Online

Why do we need the Internet? The Internet is used for homework, doing research, reading the news, keeping in touch with friends, passing or wasting time, or just visiting a cool place. As cool as it might seem, you can also get into trouble. Just passing time online is a road to the wrong path in life. Going into sites that have been prohibited is wrong since that's where you meet all kinds of characters.

Let's examine how you can get in trouble. While surfing online, there are advertisements that pop up. Most of these pop-ups have messages that push you towards wanting to find out more. Venturing into these sites means there is a great chance that they might want you to give your personal information before being allowed access. Giving personal information online to someone you don't know is dangerous. Information asked is not limited to name, address, hobbies, social security number, and family members. What this means is that you might be giving information to a predator, thief, or even a gang member. Fraud is also being committed by people who come across your personal information. Shows on television examine how predators catch their prey online. Most of these conversations might start off as simply as saying hello. The more you engage in it, the more it becomes heated. Remember, good girls have fallen victim to predators; it takes a smart girl to know what to do. Don't engage in a conversation with a stranger online. Even though he might say he is a certain age, you cannot determine age online.

Chat rooms, Facebook, and Twitter are places that people meet to exchange personal information by way of writing or pictures. More chat rooms might pop up that are not familiar. These chat rooms are not governed by any laws; at the same time, the owners of these sites have a tendency to take them down or switch names instantly. There is so much going on that it is not easy to track each site. Be cautious and research a site before getting involved.

Webcams are becoming more and more common. You can visit the whole world with a webcam. How safe this is it depends on what kind of information you are transmitting and to whom. Safe measures have to be followed.

How to Protect Yourself Online

If you see anything that you don't recognize, don't answer or try to find out. Surf smart by remaining as anonymous as possible; don't give out personal information. You can create an email address that uses a nickname instead of your real name just to use when you surf the Web. If they insist on having more information, leave the site and find another way out if it means that much to you.

Cyber Bullying

This is something that anyone with an email address or who surfs online gets. These messages are threatening, strange, irritating, frightening, and unknown. Some of these negative messages come from friends; ignore them and don't answer. These kinds of messages are also texted to cell phones. Normally, the numbers are blocked.

Blogs and Video Clips

These are another type of frightening and irritating pop-ups that you might see while online. These video clips are such a nuisance and won't go off with one click. You have to keep on trying to take it off again. Just ignore them.

Installing age-appropriate parental controls blocks computer hackers from sending you offensive messages, and advertisements. Spam blockers will keep your email from being hacked and will also detect spam mail.

Don't download files if you don't recognize or know the sender. Delete them without opening them to avoid getting a virus. You will need to purchase virus software to help you rid your computer of unwanted spyware. These programs report what your computer is doing; keep this software updated as new technology evolves.

If you see anything suspicious, report it immediately, tell an adult, or call a friend. As usual, remember that it has to be someone you know and trust. Anytime you go online for any reason, do exercise common sense and caution. A smart girl chooses what is right.

Exercising To Stay Healthy

According to the United States Surgeon General, seventeen percent of teenagers ages twelve to nineteen and nineteen percent of children ages six to eleven years are overweight. This is mainly due to lack of exercise or too little exercise and poor nutrition. Healthy eating and exercising are the only way to maintain a healthy weight. More teens are spending more time on the computer or television.

The motivation to get and stay comes from within. You need to stay motivated to keep on going. Workout with friends. Always carry your workout bag with you. Schedule exercise sessions each week. Keep track of your exercises each day.

Be committed, and if you fail to exercise one day, it won't hurt. Just go back to the routine the following day. Don't set unrealistic goals. Goals need to be realistic and achievable.

Diets pills are harmful to your metabolism. They promise a quick fix and no permanent changes are made. The goal is to develop an exercise routine, eat a balanced diet, and stay healthy. Diet pills have been linked to heart diseases, dependency, etc. Use of harmful supplements is not needed for you to get lean, strong, toned, and healthy.

There is no perfect exercise for you to lose weight, be strong, or stay healthy. Exercise regularly at least sixty minutes a day. Start with moderate activities and work your way up to more vigorous exercises.

Types of Exercises

Aerobic Exercises

Aerobic exercises are done to accomplish individual goals. They improve blood circulation and transportation of oxygen in the body, reduce blood circulation, and burn fat. These can be simple exercises like walking, cycling, swimming, running, and engaging in group sports. These exercises should be done at least three times a week. Walking is a good, simple exercise that burns up calories. Skating can be fun, so can going out to swim with friends. Doing chores around the house burns up calories. Buy an exercise video that you can do in the house; this will help you stay motivated especially when the weather does not allow you to go outdoors.

Anaerobic Exercises

Anaerobic exercises are good for building strength, endurance, stamina, muscle mass, speed, power, and metabolic rate. They concentrate on burning calories when the body is at rest.

Types of exercises in the anaerobic category include push-ups, tug of war, sit-ups, and squats. Power lifting exercises are not recommended as they can cause injury.

Excessive exercising is also not recommended. It causes changes in the menstrual cycle and bone loss. Refrain from setting unrealistic goals. Strength can be built at any age. You cannot control what you cannot change. Dramatic weight loss does not occur overnight. Safe weight loss is a slow process. Unhealthy diets to speed up the process often backfire.

What to Eat to Stay Healthy

According to the department of agriculture, the following guidelines should help you understand what foods to eat and why they are important to your overall health.

Carbohydrates. The body breaks down carbohydrates into simple sugars, which provide energy. There are two types of carbohydrates simple and complex. Simple carbohydrates are also called simple sugars and are found in refined products like white flour and its products. Nutritious foods with sugars include milk and fruit. The best way to get simple sugars is from milk and fruit because they contain vitamins, fiber, and nutrients. Complex carbohydrates are also called starches. These are found in grain products such as bread, crackers, and pasta. Processed grains such as white flour and rice have the nutrients and fiber removed. Fiber makes you feel full so you won't overeat.

Protein comes from beef, poultry, beans, and lentils. It builds up, maintains, and replaces the tissues in your body muscles, organs, and immune system. Your body uses protein to make specialized protein molecules for specific jobs. Protein is used to make hemoglobin, the part of the red blood cells that carries oxygen to every part of the body. Other proteins are used to build cardiac muscles. Bake, broil, or grill meats and beans. Vary your choices with more fish, beans, peas, and nuts. Nuts also contain healthy oils.

Vitamins and minerals are found in fruits and vegetables that are rich in different nutrients.

You need to eat at least three ounces of whole grain, bread, cereal, crackers, rice or pasta every day in order to meet your grain quota. Look for the word whole.

Vegetables are necessary, but the amount needed per day depends on the age and level of physical activity. Girls eight years old and younger need one to one-and-a-half cups of vegetables daily. Girls ages nine to thirteen need two cups daily and girls ages fourteen to eighteen need two and a half cups of vegetables daily. Any vegetable or 100 percent vegetable juice, raw or cooked, fresh, frozen, dried, whole or smashed is recommended.

Eat a variety of fruits—fresh, frozen, canned, or dried—daily.

Milk and other dairy products provide calcium. If you can't consume milk, choose lactose-free products or other calcium sources.

Types of oils include canola oil, corn, cottonseed, olive, safflower oil, soybean, and sunflower oil. These should be eaten in moderation.

It is very important that you eat a well balanced diet. There is a difference between eating a balances diet, skipping meals, and eating too much. Every age group has portions based on recommended caloric intake. Skipping meals to lose weight slows down metabolism. Eating less might mean not having enough nutrients that the body needs. Skipping meals just makes you hungry and chances are you might end up eating more the next time you do sit at a dinner table.

Following a diet plan is too much stress for one to take. Some of these diets come as frozen food or mean eating nearly the same thing every day. This is so boring and much difficult at a younger age to follow. Drinking of shakes as substitutes for a meal might work for a while. The problem is that some of these shakes don't have the necessary vitamins and nutrients. Some have a different kind of taste that you might like for a while, but not like later. Drink plenty of water.

In order to lose weight, exercise and eating healthfully are the keys. Keep an exercise routine. Stick with it and be motivated from the inside out. Have friends who can be exercise buddies and encourage you to keep on going. No miracles should be expected, but it will take hard work. The more you exercise, the easier it becomes.

Summary

We have looked at several things that make you a smart girl. We have eliminated every negative aspect and looked at different ways of dealing with normal, everyday issues. These are challenges that many face or that you might be up against now or in the future. How you tackle and deal with every one of them is what makes you a smart girl.

The media can be a positive tool for learning if positive information is transmitted. A lot of times the media tends to transmit what is viewed as ratings and not the impact it has on the viewers. Newspapers and magazines are doing the same thing.

Through the media, we came face to face with topics like how to catch a predator using real life examples. It shows child predators of all ages and professions. Even though most of the predators knew that the person they were talking to was a minor, they kept on going forward with chatting. Online chatting is a big heat on the Internet. Predators will use every kind of way to try to lure the victims. Most of these men were bold, inconsiderate, and didn't even have respect for people's homes, neighborhoods, or communities.

Discovery channel is the girls' pick. There is no limit on what you can learn or will learn. Most girls have watched programs that have opened a different world and understanding of real-life values. Most of us have traveled the world through this channel. Knowledge is the key; keep on learning.

The food network sets the foundation for the girls to learn how to cook from their kitchens right at home. This is a great motivation and inspiration. Educational channels like Houston PBS continue to inspire and teach people of all ages. These are just few examples; there several others that are making a big difference.

Early pregnancy, sexually transmitted diseases, HIV, and AIDS are on the rise. With proper teaching and spreading the word through advertising and campaigns, this message will reach every community. These risks will be reduced.

Online dating is now being used by sexual predators and child molesters to lure young girls. Young girls are meeting people online who have promises of a better future or who are promising to buy them things they need. A proper parental control is needed by purchasing software that blocks these sites. This will make online surfing safe for minors.

Text messaging is now linked to accidents and health problems. Too many teenagers are spending time text messaging. It is also comes with a financial cost to the parents.

Alcohol and drug abuse are major issues facing our teens today. Driving under the influence or riding in a car that is being driven by a drunken person is putting your life at risk. Someone drunk is not in a position to make clear judgments or to control the car. So many families today that have lost a loved one due to drunk driving or being hit by a drunk driver. Don't at anytime think that just the fact that you don't drink and drive makes it okay. We are all at risk of drunk drivers. Millions have lost lives due to drunk driving. The best thing is to spread the message and follow the rules.

Cigarette smoking is a health risk. It is linked to lung cancer and addictions. In the United States alone, the number of teens smoking has risen, even with the higher taxes on cigarettes. Most of this is linked to heavy advertising and commercials coupled with peer pressure. Quit smoking or never take the first smoke; it is a habit that is hard to stop.

Abuse of prescription medications has now become a big epidemic. Prescription medications have long been known to kill people, but now it is increasing at an alarming rate. More people are dying due to the misuse of prescription medications. More teens have or are taking prescription medications for non-medical reasons. This is due to easy availability through peers and malpractice by some medical doctors who have no respect for their careers or moral ethics. Online purchases with a credit card make getting prescriptions easy. Anyone with ten dollars can own a Visa prepaid credit card. Television advertisements say specifically what every drug does plus the symptoms for which they are used. Anyone that gives you drugs, be it prescription drugs or street drugs, does not meet the definition of a friend. A friend is someone who loves and cares about you. So, how can someone who cares about you want to harm you?

Dating comes with a lot of responsibilities. Recognize the signs of abuse: emotional, psychological, physical, or verbal. It starts small, but might end up tragically. Get out of this relationship and seek help through family, friends, and counseling. Take this stand; it is the right thing to do.

To lose weight, you have to exercise and eat healthfully. Eating too much and not exercising do not help to you lose weight. There numerous diets and diet pills on the market. These promise quick results, but don't last. Set up an exercise routine and try to keep it going. Keep motivated by having exercise buddies and know that size doesn't matter. You are a beautiful person; what matters is the inside.

Going green brings us to one of the most talked-about topics. From generating other sources of energy into energy-efficient cars, to greenhouses, to conserving the environment and marine life, we all need to start going green. We can organize our communities to set up recycling centers. We can take up projects within our homes and with our neighbors that involve building, gathering, and cultivating such as building backyard poultry houses and cultivating gardens to grow fruits and vegetables. Gather things that you no longer use in the house and donate them to a charity or companies that do recycle, or have a garage sale. Be careful not to dump or trash the neighborhood or the environment.